MISSING PIECES

Mitchell Jr.

TABLE OF CONTENTS

BIO

MARC MITCHELL JR. WAS BORN IN HAMMOND, INDIANA. AT THE AGE OF 9 HIS MOM MOVED TO ILLINOIS. ALONG WITH 3 OTHER SIBLINGS AND HIMSELF. MARC WENT TO SCHOOL AT CRETE ELEMENTARY FOR ONE YEAR, UNTIL MARC'S MOTHER MADE THE DECISION TO MOVE TO THE NEXT TOWN, "PARK FOREST". FOR TWO YEARS MARC WENT TO MOHAWK ELEMENTARY. FROM THERE MARC WENT TO, WHAT USED TO BE CALLED "FOREST TRAIL", (MICHELLE OBAMA MIDDLE SCHOOL). MARC GRADUATED FROM THAT MIDDLE SCHOOL TO LATER ATTEND RICH EAST HIGH-SCHOOL IN 2016. MARC PLAYED BASKETBALL HIS FRESHMAN YEAR AND ON THE "B TEAM" AVERAGED A DOUBLE DOUBLE (10PPG 10 RPG) AS A STARTER. ON THE "A TEAM HE AVERAGED 9RPG BUT MARC DIDN'T GET THE PT (PLAYING TIME) HE DESERVED. MARC HAS ALWAYS BEEN A STUDENT FIRST, ATHLETE SECOND. HE FINISHED

FRESHMAN YEAR WITH A 3.2 GPA. THE NEXT YEAR MARC HAD A 3.0 GPA. BASKETBALL WISE WAS A CRAZY YEAR FOR HIM BUT HE HIT A BUZZER BEATER FOR THE WIN VS RICH SOUTH DURING THE SEASON. IN ADDITION TO ALL OF THAT MARC IS NOT AN AVERAGE 17 YEAR OLD. HE HAS BEEN TRAINED BY AUTHOR AGEE IN 2011. ALSO IN 2011 WAS WHEN MARC JOINED B.O.B WITH THE MAGIC JOHNSON FOUNDATION. IN 2014, MARC WAS TRAINED BY N.B.A LEGEND BILL CARTWRIGHT. IN 2017 MARC WAS TRAINED AND COACHED BY N.B.A LEGEND CRAIG HODGES. CURRENTLY MARC IS WITH THE ILLINOIS BOCATS AAU BASKETBALL TEAM. (2019) OUTSIDE OF BASKETBALL HE HELPS FEED THE HOMELESS EVERY-NOW AND THEN WITH MICHAEL AIRHEART AT EVENTS LIKE THE TASTE FOR THE HOMELESS.

The best feeling in the world is when everyone loves you.

The day when these characters hard work and dedication

paid off they felt that feeling. Morris is a suburban kid from

south state. He doesn't care what people thinks about him.

He just wants to change the world. People think that he

can't do it. People used to talk about him, call him names,

bum, ugly, stinky, lame. They think he won't be anything

in life. Well, he doesn't care. In his mind he says "why

can't they just support me? I would've supported them if

they were doing something." Morris's mom taught him the

right way to live life and so far he has done that. He says

ma'am, sir, and opens the doors for women. One lady said

"you are doing great sir keep listening to your mother and

anything you want in life, anything you want to do,

anything you desire will be yours!" Wow! How many kids

you know an adult would say such thing to. Morris is only

16! He has a long, long, long way to go.

Morrison Michael is a suburban boy from Hammond,

Indiana. Moo-Moo wasn't a natural Hooper. Morris

actually was more into tech as a kid. When Moo was about

seven years old he played games on his family member's

phone. He played the video game on his brother's game-

system. As a child he loved his family and his family loved

him. But the love was MOSTLTY from his mother. His

mom was always there for him. In Indiana, he lived with

his mom, big sister Nae-Nae, big brother Bookie and soon

to be little sister Lilmama. Everybody in the house loved

Moo-Moo's energy. He was always hyper as any seven

year old would be. His mom owned the house they called the "Green-house". They called it that because one; it was the best house they had ever been in, and two it was painted green. All of them had lots of fun together. Especially in their backyard during the summer. As Morris got older he got wiser, smarter, and taller. Moo-moo still is the same person. He still is caring, loving and respectful. But he is careful when it comes to people period. Lots of people tried to break this kid apart from what he is destined to be. Let's start with Father. His dad was in and out of his life. His dad says all time "I love you mane" but when he was in town he didn't even call him. He didn't even come and see him. He would call his mother and say "Hey I'm in town for one day I'll pick him up and drop him off later". His mom would asked "Do you want to go?" and of course he would say "yea!!" His mom knew he would be disappointed because it's been 2 years since he seen him and that was at a funeral. Now he is just going to take him for one day to buy his love? Morris didn't know any better he just was glad to see his dad like any kid would. So as Moo-moo became a teen he stared to realize what his mother was saying was true "I'm sorry but yo daddy aint' shit". On to the next family member. Nae-Nae. The oldest you would think she would be the good example but nope. When she was in college she was not living on campus she still lived with mama. One day Mama bought her a car. She loved it but all Nae-nae had to do was get her license. She didn't get it. In fact she got a boyfriend who has one. She wanted him to drive for her but the only problem is that the car is still in mama's name. So when Nae-nae was going to get her license mama was going to put it her name. On top of

that her boyfriend smoked weed in the car! So mama and

Nae-Nae fell out. Ever since she never called and

apologized or even check up on her siblings.

Chapter 2: UP Next?

Bill is not an everyday regular teen. He was born in the

suburbs where they can play some ball. Half of the people

out there had fundamentals the other half was street ball.

Bill wasn't a hooper until he enter the 5th grade. He always liked basketball but never took it serious. His first practice he went to he felt nervous. Everybody was more experienced or a little bit higher in knowledge than Bill. They were like family, some of his teammates were nice but about one or two were arrogant and mean. The difference between Bill and the other players is 1; he is long and most of all, hard working. He didn't know anything about work ethic or getting recruited. He just wanted to play ball. Even though Bill didn't work out in the gym daily or dribble outside every day, he was in the gym practicing every day. Working on his shot, his form, his dribbling, EVERY, SINGLE, DAY. And even though he wasn't the strongest; wasn't the smartest on the court maybe tied with speed and quickness but the fact is he worked hard. So when it was time to play he was ready. He knew all of the plays. At this point he just wanted to play basketball and go straight to the league when he gets older! This was his dream. He wants to accomplish it. Will he? Is it possible that a child from Indiana (moved to Illinois) that doesn't know much about the game. Someone doesn't have anyone to teach him more about it. Has no father figure to help him. Just his mother and sister to support him make it that far? Not a chance right!? Well stay tuned in and pay close attention. One day Bill woke up, he couldn't wait until this afternoon. It was game day for the thunder. First, Bill took a shower then he prayed, last he ate. He had cinnamon toast crunch. So before the game his mother had to go buy groceries because the fridge was empty. When they arrived at the store Bill had a vision. He has vision on the daily basis and his mother says "God gives us visions to show us what's going to happen before it does." So what the vision was just his team losing the game today. And Bill tweaked out he said "MOM MOM MOM". She said "WHAT BILL". He said "WE GOING TO LOOSE TODAY." in his sad voice. His mom said, "That isn't the spirit Bill you...." "No I had a vision and the vision was we were going to lose our game today." She said "aw it's going to be ok baby just focus on winning today." "Ok mom." And Bill and his mother went in the car and drove off. So when they arrived, everyone was there. The coaches, the players, the refs, and the parents of the players. All of a sudden Bill caught the butterflies. Surprisingly, Bill's step dad came to the game. He watches Bill every day. He might as well be bill's real dad. Anyways Bill is in the starting lineup this game and he is playing power forward because he is long, skinny and fast. Bill showed a lot of hustle during this game. A lot of heart coming from an 11 year old. Bill just wanted to show everyone how much love he has for this game. How much basketball means to him. And he did but the team didn't. So Bill was right... They were going to lose the game and they did. Bill had 3rb 5pts 3ast 2stls. That good for a person who just started to hoop. So his "dad" said "It's alright son. You'll get 'em next time. "All this did was motive him more to practice every day.

Work on his craft every day. His goal was to prove everyone wrong. Let's see if he will accomplish it.......

Chapter 3 Mature & Tryouts

Bill is 13 now, and in 8th grade and he wants to try out for his first school team. Tryouts is in October. Bill is focused and ready to work hard. So when October hit Bill showed up. Everybody was so good. A lot of people were stronger, taller, quicker, any trait you could think of the majority of them was better in except 3. Heart, Hustle, and humbled. Those 3 traits made Bill stand out a little bit more than most players at the tryouts. After the last day of tryouts (day 3) Bill just made it. He was close to the bottom of the list!! His coach said "you almost didn't make it." in his joking voice. But Bill didn't think he was kidding when he said that. He kept his cool though. Afterwards, Bill goes to school and attends all of his classes. All day he is thinking about his first practice after-school. When the day ended all of his teammates went straight to the gym. So Bill went with them. This is the very first practice and the coach says loudly "All of you are out of shape!!!!" Instantly everybody looked at each other. Then coach said "ON THE LINE." So they all got on the baseline. Then he said "GO." Now Bill has no idea what is going on. But he is very smart so he assumes that he needs to run with the rest of the team. And he did. After that practice everyone was about to pass out, or was out of breath. Bill did not complain he didn't kept going even though he was exhausted. This wa

days Bill just wanted to lay down and relax

Bill did the same thing he did yesterday. He went to se

Did all of his work. Had to listen to people talking about

him. All of that he went through every day for 1 more

school year. One more year and he is in high school. All

Bill wants to do is make his mother proud and prove

everyone wrong. So as the days fly by and Bill still has the

same role (bench player). Bill starts to be really upset. But

it motivates him to work even harder on his game. And

guess what? He did. He spent countless hours in the gym

just trying to get better. He wants to be able to reach new

heights. He wants to be the best. He wants to be able to

dibble great, pass greater, and be unstoppable. All of this

and the coach doesn't give him a chance. The coach or the

teammates doesn't even help him out or give him tips on

how to improve his game. Its every player for themselves

instead of lets help our teammate so we can all be great and ual. So he had to accept that. Every day he went through some type of problem. One day it's something outside of basketball, another it could be he is having an off day. Bill would miss more than half of his shots in practice and feel terrible. This shows how much he really cares about the game of basketball. He is the best example of a "real Hooper". The days of Bills 8th grade basketball season went by really fast. And the coach didn't give a care if god gave him a brain and a heart. During the last days of the season Bill received more minutes than he ever did on that team. He didn't care about his numbers, he just wanted to play and help his team win. They won that game, and Bill felt a little better knowing he contributed in a team win. Time flies and its August. Time for a new school. High school. As Bill enters his new school with his mom for registration he feels something. Something like he could belong or fit in with this school. He was nervous and shy talking to staff and students that attend their now. As Bill and his mother walked towards the back of the school Bill heard a familiar sound. And his mother already knew....

Basketball. So they followed the sound of basketballs pounding. When they make it to the back there are lots of people hooping. The coach is there and former members of the school. Bill asked "So what's going on in here" To the coach for varsity and he said "Open gym you tryna' play?" Bill looked at him mom. His mom looked at him and said "Go ahead Bill", Bill was so excited he gets to play in his new school before tryouts start. This is all new to him. So Bill puts on his gear and went to show what he got.

Compared to everyone in the gym Bill was the less knowledgeable one of them all. Everybody knew a lot. They Was bigger, stronger, smarter, maybe even better. And the varsity coach pulled him to the other side of the court and improved his jump shot. He taught him how to shoot properly instead of just throwing it up hoping that it would go in.

Bill is a very smart kid. He is respectful, kind and obedient. The only thing that changed is his age and him maturity. By the time he reached his freshman year in high school, he was mature enough to know what's right and what's wrong. Something some teens in his generation do not care about. His sister and his mother were his only family.

One day they all went to a facility to feed the less fortunate people. Often is when they do this. TO ADD TO THAT THEY ALSO HELP PARENTS WHO CAN'T AFFORD TO BUY THEIR CHILDREN CHRISTMAS PRESENTS. IT'S AND ORGANIZATION CALLED "THE BLOCK". THAT ORGANIZATION DOES NUMEROUS OF OTHER EVENTS. THEY HELP THE COMMUNITY BY BUILDING PARKS. THEY PASS OUT CLOTHS, FOOD, AND PERSONAL NEEDS.

NOW RECENTLY BILL AND HIS SISTER IS

NOMINATED FOR AN AWARD. THE AWARD IS

FROM "THE BLOCK". THEY ARE THE MOST

SUPPORTIVE KIDS IN THAT ORGANIZATION. OF

COURSE THEIR MOTHER IS VERY PROUD AND

EXCITED.WHEN THEY ARIVE THEIR ARE PEOPLE

RECORDING, PEOPLE PLAYING BASKETBALL, ALL

OF THE ABOVE. NOW THIS IS WHAT REALLY

MAKES BILL DIFFERENT FROM THE OTHER TEENS.

FOR ONE HE TREATS ADULTS WITH RESPECT. NOT

A-LOT OF TEENS YOU CAN SEE THAT ACTUALLY

SHOWS SOME REPECT TO EVEN THEIR PARENTS. IF

THE PARENTS WOULD STOP TRYING TO BE THEIR

CHILDS FREIND, AND BE THEIR PARENT THE

WORLD WOULD BE A LOT DIFFERENT.

BILL NEVER SAGGED, (THAT ONE TIME HE LEFT HIS BELT AT HOME DON'T COUNT). HE DOESN'T FOLLOW ANYBODY. HE RIDES HIS OWN WAVE.

CHAPTER 5

BILL WAS APART OF ANOTHER ORGANIZATION
CALLED EVERYBODY MATTERS. WHAT THEY DO
IS SLIGHTLY DIFFERENT FROM WHAT THE BLOCK
DOES. BUT COMPLETELY DIFFERENT. BILL AND
HIS FAMILY WENT WITH THIS ORGANIZATION
ONE DAY. THEY WENT TO THE SCIENCE INDUSTRY
AND CHANCE THE RAPPER WAS THERE. THE
ORGANIZATION HAD MASCOTS FOR HIM AND
SOME OTHERS TO PUT ON. WHEN BILL TRIED IT ON
IT WAS REALLY HARD TO SEE. EVENTUALLY HE
GOT USED TO IT AND HE BEGAN TO GET THE HANG
OF BEING A MASCOT.

THEY WENT AROUND THE WHOLE MUSEUM AND FLASHES WERE COMING LEFT AND RIGHT. INSTANTLY IT BECAME HOT. IT DIDN'T HELP THAT HE WAS DANCING AND EVERYTHING TOO. GOOD THING HIS MOTHER WAS ACCOMPANYING HIM. AFTER ABOUT AN HOUR, THEY WENT BACK TO THE SPOT THEY MET UP AT. ALL OF THE MASCOTS ARE SWEATING, INCLUDING BILL. THEY'VE FINISHED THEIR GOOD DEED. BILL WAS MICHAEL JORDAN. THE OTHERS CONSISTED OF COOKIE MONSTER, HAPPY EMOJI, QUAVO, MOANA, AND OTHERS.

ANOTHER EVENT THAT BILL ATTENDED IN IS THE TASTE OF THE HOMELESS EVENT. IN THAT EVENT THEY HELPED THE HOMELESS ABUNDANTLY. THE CEO OF ALL KIDS MATTER HAD SUPPORT FROM A CELEB AND WAS ABLE TO GET 30 COACH BUSES

TO PICK HOMELESS PEOPLE UP AND BRING THEM TO THEIR LOCATION! AT THE EVENT THEY HAD FREE CLOTHS, FREE FOOD, FREE ENTERTAINMENT, EVEN FREE HAIRCUTS! THE EVENT WAS VERY SUCCESSFUL. THEY GAVE AWAY JORDANS AND IPHONES TO THE PEOPLE WHO NEEDED IT! THE CEO AND CO-CEO ARE HUSBAND AND WIFE. THEY ARE VERY GOOD PEOPLE AND THEY TREAT EVERYONE LIKE FAMILY.

CHAPTER 6:

BILL

BILL- MEANS DETERMINED PROTECTOR/WILLIAM.

BILL IS ALWAYS PROTECTIVE WHEN IT COMES TO
HIS MOTHER OR HIS REAL FAMILY. YOU CAN
PROBABLY GUESS WHAT ELSE HE IS PROTECTIVE

OVER. BASKETBALL. WHEN IT COMES TO BASKETBALL YOU HAVE TO KNOW WHAT YOU ARE TALKING ABOUT. BECAUSE IF YOU DON'T HE WILL GET VERY DEFENSIVE. BACK TO HIS CAREER. BILL HAD ONE MOMENT WHERE HE CRIED BECAUSE OF BASKETBALL. LITTLE DOES HE KNOW THERE WILL BE MORE TIMES LIKE THAT? SO ITS 10 SECONDS LEFT AND BILL GOT FOULED HES AT THE FREE THROW LINE. REMIND THAT HE IS IN HIGH-SCHOOL SO HE GETS ONE AND ONES. IF HE MISSES THE FIRST THEN THE PLAY IS NOW ACTIVE BUT IF HE MAKES IT THEN HE GETS ANOTHER. SO HE TAKES HIS TWO DRIBBLES HE SHOOTS........ AND HE MISSED! THE OTHER TEAM GETS THE REBOUND AND BILL FOULS. AS THEY HEAD TO THE OTHER SIDE FOR THE OTHER TEAMS FREE-THROWS, BILLS EMOTIONS ARE GOING CRAZY IN HIS BODY. WHEN THE GAME IS OVER HE

GOES IN LINE TO SAY GOOD GAME AND SHAKE THE OPPOSING TEAMS HAND HE BEGAN TO CRY AND AFTER HE SHOCKED THEIR HAND HE WENT TO THE LOCKER ROOM AND WAS CRYING. IT WASN'T THAT SAD CRY IT WAS THAT MAD CRY. HIS MOTHER SAID "YOU DID THE BEST YOU COULD, IT SHOULD'VE GOTEN TO THE POINT WHERE THE GAME WAS THAT CLOSE YOU WANT WIN IT BY YOURSELF!"

CHAPTER 7

SOPHOMORE

WHEN BILL WAS FINISHED WITH HIS FRESHMAN
SEASON HE INSTANTLY WENT TO THE GYM
ALMOST EVERYDAY AFTER! HE SAID "IM GOING
TO COME BACK AND I WILL BE IN THE STARTING
LINEUP AND GET MY FIRST DUNK." SO HE

WORKED HARD THROUGH THE WHOLE SUMMER. HE DID SHOOTING DRILLS, DRIBBLING DRILLS, AND CONDITIONING. DAYS GO BY AND THE SUMMER IS PASSING BY. AND BEFORE HE KNEW IT, IT WAS ALMOST TIME FOR TRYOUTS! TRYOUTS IS IN NOVEMBER ITS OCTOBER 29.

BILL HAD A 3.4 GPA AND HE START SLACKING TOWARDS TRYOUTS! BY TRYOUTS BILL HAD A 2.3 GPA! HE WAS SUPER DISAPPOINTED IN HIMSELF. THE DIFFERENCE BETWEEN BILL AND OTHER BOYS IN HIS SCHOOL IS THAT OTRHER BOYS WOULD JUST LEAVE IT AT THAT OR LET IT GET WORSE. BILL KEPT HIS HEAD UP AND CONTINUED TO IMPROVE HIS GPA.

IN ORDER TO TRYOUT, YOU NEED AT LEAST A 2.0 GPA. BILL MADE THE SOPHOMORE TEAM! BUT THERE WAS ONE PROBLEM, HE COULDN'T PLAY IN THE FIRST 3 GAMES. HE WENT BELOW A 2.0 GPA!

GOOD THING THE GAMES WERE TOURNAMENT
GAMES SO THEY DIDN'T COUNT TOWARDS THEIR
REGULAR SEASON RECORD.

CHAPTER 8 FIRST GAME AS A SOPHOMORE

SO AS BILL GOT HIS GPA UP, THE TEAM
CONTINUED TO STRUGGLE. THEIR NEXT GAME
BILL WAS ELIGIBLE TO PLAY. HE IS PUT AT POWER
FOWARD/SMALL FOWARD. IN THE 2QUATER,
COACH PUT BILL IN. THE FIRST PLAY BILL MAKES
IS ON DEFENSE HE GETS A STEAL, AND PASSES IT
PASS HALF COURT TO HIS TEAMMATE WHO WAS
FOULED. THIS GAME IS A TORNEY GAME BUT,

THEY STILL WANT TO WIN THIS FOR THE TROPHY TO PUT IT IN THE SCHOOL.

SO BILLS TEAM ENDED UP LOOSING IN THE SECOND ROUND TO THE BLUE SEALS. BILL DIDN'T GET A LOT OF PLAYING TIME AS HE WANTED TO SO HE COULDN'T CONTRIBUTE TO THE TEAM!

BILL IS HIGHLY UPSET THAT FOR ONE, THEY LOST THEIR TORNEY AND FOR TWO, HE DIDN'T GET ENOUGH PLAYING TIME TO CONTRIBUTE. BILL SAID TO MOM "IT'S NOT FAIR MOM I PRACTICE HARDER THAN EVERYBODY ON THE TEAM." MOM SAID "IT'S OKAY BILL JUST TALK TO HIM AND ASK HIM WHAT YOU NEED TO WORK ON." BILL SAID "OK."

CHAPTER 9:

THE TALK

BILL IS A SHY KID IN A LOUD PERSONS BODY. HE
TALKS A LOT BUT IN REALITY HE IS SHY TO SAY
STUFF. THIS IS THE DAY. THIS IS THE DAY BILL
WILL STEP UP AND BE A UP STANDER. THE BUCKS
AND BILL HAVE PRACTICE TODAY. BILL WILL BE
BRAVE TODAY AND ASK THE QUESTION. SO THE
COACH IS OUTSIDE OF THE GYM, IN THE SCHOOL
HALLWAY AND BILL SAYS "WASSUP COACH."
COACH SAID "WASSUP BILL."

BILL COULDN'T DO IT! HE WAS TO NERVOUS SHY
AND FELT LIKE HE WAS UNDER PRESSURE. SO
AFTER PRACTICE HE HAD ANOTHER CHANCE TO

ASK HIM AND GUESS WHAT HE SAID?! HE SAID "

HEY COACH, WHAT TIME IS PRACTICE

TOMMARO?" COACH SAID "10:30" BILL EXITED THE

GYM.

WHEN BILL GOT HOME HIS MOTHER SAID "SO

WHAT DID HE SAY?" BILL SAID" I COULDN'T MOM I

WAS TOO SCARED." "SO YOU JUST GONNA' BE

SCARED ALL YOUR LIFE? WHEN YOU GO TO THE

N.B.A MILLIONS OF PEOPLE WOULD BE WATCHING

AND YOU COULD BE IN THIS SAME SITUATION."

MOM SAID "SO WHAT ARE YOU GOING TO DO?"

BILL SAID "I WILL DO IT TOMORROW." MOM SAID"

BECAUSE IM NOT THE ONE PLAYING

BASKETBALL, YOU ARE.

CHAPTER 10: PRESENT

IN 2019 I JOINED THE ILLINOIS BOBCATS. AFTER NOT MAKING THE VARSITY TEAM I WAS DEVASTATED. BASKETBALL MEANS EVERYTHING TO ME AND FOR IT TO BE JUST TAKEN AWAY LIKE THAT HURT ME. BUT MY MOTHER KEPT ME GOING AND I HAD TO STAY MOTIVATED. SO ALL SUMMER I WORKED REALLY HARD. AFTER ALL, I REALIZED THAT BASKETBALL WASN'T TAKEN AWAY FROM ME. BECAUSE I HAD AAU. I HAD SUMMER CAMPS. ALSO, I HAD OPPORTUNITIES THAT PEOPLE WHO MADE THE VARSITY TEAM DIDN'T HAVE. WHICH WAS EXTRA TIME. EXTRA TIME TO GET STRONGER, FASTER, SMARTER, AND MORE

KNOWLEDGABLE. SO ALMOST EVERYDAY I HAVE
BEEN GOING TO BOBCATS PRACTICES EVERYDAY.
BEFORE AND AFTER I ALSO WORKED OUT EITHER
OUTSIDE, OR IN THE GYM. IM ALWAYS FULL OF
ENERGY, READY TO PLAY AT ALL TIMES. IN THE
TOURNAMENTS I HAD TO CHANGE THE WAY I
THINK AND PLAY WITH THEM. AFTER PLAYING
WITH THEM I LEARNED A LOT AND GAINED A LOT
OF EXPERIENCE FROM PLAYING IN
TOURNAMENTS. IM STILL WITH THE BOBCATS
TILL THIS DAY. AFTER A COUPLE OF MONTHS
PLAYING WITH BOBCATS, A NEW SEASON OF
SUMMER LEAGUE BASKETBALL STARTED. AND
RICH EAST HAS A NEW COACH. COACH JD. COACH
JD DOESN'T LIKE TO LOSE. HE SAYS HE IS NOT A
LOOSER. AND HE WANTED US TO AQUIRE THE
ATTITUDE OR MINDSET THAT HE HAS. WHICH IS
TO WIN. SO FAR WE HAVE BEEN WORKING MON-

THUR 2-3 TIMES A DAY AND 2-3 HOURS EACH DAY. EVERYDAY YOU CAN SEE THAT EVERYBODY IS GETTING BETTER AS A UNIT. EVEN INDIVIDUALLY YOU CAN SEE GROWTH. NOT A LOT OF COACHES CARE ABOUT THEIR PLAYERS, OR EVEN SHOW EQUALITY TO ALL OF THEIR PLAYERS. THERE IS ALWAYS A LOT OF FAVORITISM. EVERY TEAM IVE BEEN ON IT'S ALWAYS A FAVORITE AND NO RECOGNITION. I CAN HONESTLY SAY SO FAR I SEE NO FAVORITISM IN NONE OF OUR COACHES. COACH MCGUIRE, COACH SHAE, ETC. IF YOUR HORRIBLE THAT DAY THEY ARE GOING TO TELL YOU STRAIGHT UP SO U CAN DO BETTER THAN THAT BECAUSE EVERYONE IN THE GYM IS TALENTED AND HAS SKILL. BUT THERE IS ONE THING THAT SEPARATES ME FROM EVERYBODY ELSE. I WORK THE HARDEST OUT OF EVERYBODY. EVERY TIME IM ON THE COURT NOBODY OUT

WORKS ME. EVERY COACH THAT I'VE BEEN
TRAINED BY SINCE I STARTED BASKETBALL SAID
THE SAME THING. IM THE HARDEST WORKER ON
THE TEAM! EVER SINCE 5TH GRADE IVE BEEN
WORKING CONTINUOUSLY ON MY GAME. MY
FIRST COACH, COACH VINCE HAS BEEN
WATCHING OVER HIM HIS WHOLE HIGH SCHOOL
CARRER.

CHAPTER 11: OUTSIDE OF BASKETBALL

BASKETBALL CAME SECOND BECAUSE GOD WAS
ALWAYS FIRST. MY MOM MY SISTER AND I GOES
TO FCC. FCC IS A BIG CHURCH IN MUNSTER, IN. WE

GOT BAPTIZED THERE TOGETHER. A LOT OF MY FAMILY IS NOT BLOOD. THOSE PEOPLE CHECK UP ON ME ALMOST EVERYDAY. MAKE SURE MY MOM, SISTER AND I ARE OK. THOSE PEOPLE KNOW EXACTLY WHO THEY ARE. TO BE HONEST, ALL THAT I HAVE FAMILY WISE IS MY MOTHER AND MY SISTER. THEY HAVE BEEN THERE EVERY STEP OF THE WAY. AND IT'S JUST GETTING STARTED. 2 TIMES EVERY YEAR MY FAMILY AND I GO TO THE TASTE FOR THE HOMELESS. AT THE TASTE FOR THE HOMELESS WE HELP THE HOMELESS. WE GIVE OUT FOOD, CLOTHS, AND SHOES, LITERALLY EVERYTHING YOU NEED TO SURVIVE TO SUPPORT THE HOMELESS. I USED TO BE VERY SHY. I AM A LITTLE TO AN EXTENT THOUGH. I NEVER LIKED TALKING TO PEOPLE LIKE THAT. THE WAY MY LIFE IS RIGHT NOW IF I WAS STILL SHY I WOULD BE NO WHERE IN LIFE. SO FAR I HAVE

ACCOMPLISHED SO MUCH BY SPEAKING UP. IF U CANT TALK TO PEOPLE ABOUT WHAT U DO THEN HOW WILL THEY KNOW?! YOU HAVE TO SUPORT AND PROMOTE YOURSELF EVERYDAY. UNLESS YOU WANT TO STAY UNKNOWN YOU HAVE TO SHOW THAT YOU'RE NOT A SHY PERSON. ESPECIALLY IF YOU ARE A ENTREPRENEUR. BUT HEY NOT EVERYONE HAS THE RIGHT MINDET OF WANTING TO WORK FOR THEMSELVES.

CHAPTER 12 REALITY

DO YOU REMEMBER THAT LITTLE BOY? BILL?

WOULD IT BE CRAZY IF I SAID BILL IS A REAL

CHARACTER? BILL WAS AND IS ME. THE AUTHOR.

I AM THE ONE WHO STARTED OFF PLAYING

BASKETBALL ON THE AAU LEVEL. I DON'T THINK

ANYONE YOU KNOW HAD THE OPPORTUNITIES I

HAD. TRULY I AM BLESED TO HAVE MY MOTHER

BECAUSE WITHOUT HER I WOULDN'T HAVE

THESE OPPORTUNITIES I HAVE NOW. BOOKS OVER

BALLS IS MAKING ME THE AMBASSADOR. THE

CEO FERNANDO TRUSTS ME AND MY MOTHER

ENOUGH TO BE APART OF THE BUSINESS. MY

CLOTHING LINE IS ALSO SOMETHING THAT I AM

PUTING TOGETHER RIGHT NOW. INCLUDING THIS

BOOK THAT YOU ARE CURRENTLY READING. MY

MOTHERS NAME IS TAKESHA HOWARD. SHE

PLAYED THE MOM IN THIS STORY OF COURSE AND

EVERYTHING SHE WAS SAYING, AND DOING WAS

TRUE. SHE IS THE REASON THAT IVE MADE IT THIS FAR AND SHE WILL BE THE REASON I MAKE IT TO TOP! EVERYTHING I DO I DIDN'T DO ALONE. THE CONNECTIONS MY MOTHER HAD FROM BEING AN ENTREPRENEUR WAS A BLESSING BECAUSE IT SET ME UP FOR WHATS TO COME. WE LIVE DIFFERENT FROM A LOT OF PEOPLE IN THIS WORLD ESPECIALLY TO OUR OWN BLACK PEOPLE WE ARE COMPLETELY DIFFERENT. MY MOTHER USED TO WORK 3 JOBS AT A TIME TO TRY AND FEED US, KEEP CLOTHS ON OUR BACKS, AND PAY THE BILLS. BUT IF YOU WORK A JOB CURRENTLY YOU KNOW THE STRUGGLE. YOU WOULD BE DOING ALL OF THIS WORK BUT ONLY GET PAID 9 DOLLARS AN HOUR. THEN THEY TAKE MONEY OUT YOUR CHECK AND ONLY GET PAID 200 OUT OF 2 WEEKS. WHAT IS THAT GOING TO DO WHEN YOU HAVE KIDS AND MORTGAGE TO PAY? THAT

WHY MY MOTHER HAD TO GET 3 JOBS BECAUSE WE DIDN'T HAVE FAMLIY TO HELP US OUT LIKE SOME PEOPLE DO IN THIS WORLD. WE DIDN'T HAVE A FATHER FIGURE TO HELP KEEP MONEY IN THE HOUSE. SO MOM HAD TO DO IT BY HER LONLEY. SHE CAME UP WITH A CANDY STORE AT THE HOUSE FOR EXTRA MONEY.

.

Acknowledgements

To conclude this book I would like to thank first, God. Because without god none of this would be possible without Him. Next, my mother Takesha Howard. She was my main motivator. She made sure this book was created by any means necessary. I would like to thank my little sister Carrolyn for motivating me and pushing me too. Lastly, these people supported me through the stretch and those people are; my pops, Angel Cymone, my big brother John Fulton, my friends, akia, Davion, Cj, Aj, Gilbert, Justin Moore, Amar, Kayode, Damon Stanley, Mathew Williams, Daniel, Coach Vince, Coach Lance, Author Agee, coach Craig Hodges, Coach Luke, Coach JD, Coach Shae, Coach P, Dae-Dae, Coach Stein, Malik, Darion, Brian, Steve, Ant, Daron.

About me the author:

I am Marc Mitchell Jr. I was born In Hammond, IN. My house really did burn down! That's why we moved to the south suburbs. I've lived in Hammond, East Chicago, University Park, and Park Forest. I am an African American and I'm 17 years old. My favorite color is red and black, and in my spare time I like to listen to new music and freestyle to instrumentals. I like to play video games as well as play basketball, but I play basketball all day every day. I like to help people and when I make it to the NBA I'm going to buy a facility for my mother so she can help the homeless and the needy. I think I care more about other people than myself sometimes and that can be a good and a bad thing. To be honest, I didn't think I would be writing a book. At first I thought it was lame and weird because nerds read and write books. Lol but I found out that writing a book is not as bad as people may think or it may seem. You can get a lot off your mind writing a book. Or writing in general. Whatever you do in life don't get caught up in what everybody else is doing because you can do your own thing! This generation kids are being hypnotized to believe that you HAVE to work a job. It's like everybody is programed to work a job why cant you be your own boss? Its not as hard as you think. You just have to have the mind-set of "I'm going to work as hard as i can to make this money". If your dedicated to smoking, drinking, partying, why cant you be dedicated to making money everyday, thinking of new ideas to make some money, working hard to make the money?! Just because everybody you know works a job because either; one, they're lazy. Or two, they're parents are making them, or three they don't know how to hustle. Killing yourself for 10-15$ an hour is not worth it and getting paid every two weeks. Why do that when you can do what u love to do and make a hundred a day, two hundred a day, 500 in a week. Im not trying to offend anybody or make anybody feel bad but i want to make a change in this world and i think if your reading this then you have the power to make millions! But if you think your going to make millions working a 9-5 all your life you have to come back to reality. Being and entrepreneur is not easy. It's a lot of hard-work. But it gets better.

Book Synopsis: In this story you will find out about two very similar characters, Bill, & Morrison. They go through what i would call "a different struggle". It's not as bad as the killing and murdering in chicago, but it is real deep! It shows the struggles people don't want to talk about. Lots of downfalls that lead to both characters getting back on top! At the end of this book will make you realize a lot.